To Michi and Bobby —
(two of my favorite people!)

Wishing you happiness at the holidays
...and always!

Mindy
Christmas 1993

When You Were Born in Korea

a memory book for children adopted from Korea

by Brian Boyd with photographs by Stephen Wunrow

The authors thank the dedicated staff of Eastern Child Welfare Services in Seoul for their help in making this book, and for their kindness and patience.

Thanks also to Mrs. Hyun Sook Han of the Children's Home Society of Minnesota, as well as several Children's Home adoptive parents who were especially helpful in this endeavor: Mary Fonken and Judy Tobias, whose insights and suggestions were invaluable in making this a better book than it might have been, and Theresa Utecht and Chris Murray.

We also appreciate the help provided by Mrs. Yoonju Park, Lynn Park, and the many others who were kind enough to read and comment on the manuscript.

We especially thank our wives, Cheryl Boyd and Martha Vickery, not only for their endless rereadings and helpful criticisms of the book, but as well for taking up the family load at those times when we became obsessed with this project.

To all, *kamsahamnida*.

Printed in the United States of America
97 96 95 94 93   10 9 8 7 6 5 4 3 2 1

Picture on page 6 courtesy Theresa Utecht;
lower picture on page 22 courtesy Mrs. Kim, Kwang Ok

Publisher Cataloging-in-Publication Data

Boyd, Brian
When you were born in Korea: a memory book for children adopted from Korea / Brian Boyd with photographs by Stephen Wunrow.
p.   cm.
ISBN 0-9638472-0-1
1. Korean American children - Juvenile literature.
2. Adopted children - United States - Juvenile literature.
[1. Adoption. 2. Korean Americans.]
I. Wunrow, Stephen, ill. II. Title

HV 875.64.B692 1993 362.7'34

When You Were Born in Korea

A Memory Book for Children Adopted from Korea

ISBN 0-9638472-0-1

Yeong & Yeong Book Company
1368 Michelle Drive
St. Paul, Minnesota 55123

For the foster mothers, the social workers, the doctors and nurses, and the many others who had a part in caring for all our children, and in bringing them to their moms and dads.

And especially for the birthmothers.

To Cheryl, and Sarah Po and
Anna Soo; what a nice family!
— BB

To Martha and our two miracle
daughters, one by adoption and
one by birth. — SGW

Sometimes you might wonder about yourself, and who you are, and where you came from, and how you happen to be a member of your family when you don't particularly look like your mom and dad. Families can be formed in many ways, and adoption is a great way to give families to children. Many other moms and dads have children adopted from Korea, so your family is very much like thousands of other families.

Some children wonder about who they were *before* they became part of their family. You might have a photo album that starts with pictures of your airport arrival. Did you ever wonder about what happened to you from when you were born until the time you got to the airport, and home to your family? The story of the first part of your life is really very interesting.

When you were born in Korea, there were many caring people who helped you along the way to your family. They were very important to you then, although you were too young at the time to know just how much they meant to you.

This book has the sort of pictures that could have been in your photo album, if someone had been there with a camera from your birth until you came to your family. You will see the kinds of people and places you may have experienced. Most of all, you may appreciate the love and concern you received from these people, who knew you even before your mom and dad first saw you.

Many of them still think of you now, and care very much that you are happy and healthy and growing in the love of your family.

You owe the *very* beginning of your story to the two people who gave you the gift of life: your birthmother and birthfather. They were probably two people who loved one another, and together they made a baby that was you. They may have had a difficult situation in their lives at that time, and they realized that they would not be able to care for a baby. It's hard to understand why parents would feel they couldn't raise their own child. Perhaps they were just too young to be parents, or maybe one of them died, or they had separated, or they had some other hardship that made their situation very difficult for them, and nearly impossible for a baby.

In most cases, it is really up to the birthmother to face her situation alone. The birthfather often leaves the matter to the mother, who then has to decide what is best for her baby and for herself. Sometimes she just doesn't know what to do, or where to get help. She knows that most people in her culture, even her own family, will not provide the understanding and support she and her baby need. She wants her child to have a good family and a happy life. Her wish can be realized by arranging some way for an adoption agency to take care of her baby, but this means saying good-bye to her baby, forever. This is a very hard decision for a birthmother to make.

Once she made her decision, your birthmother might have taken you to a train station or police station or some other public place, where she could be certain that you would be found immediately. The police would then take you to an orphanage or adoption agency. Or she might have gone to social workers, so she could receive help for herself as well as for you.

There may be many different ways and many different reasons for a mother to get her baby into an orphanage or an adoption agency. Her most important reason was her love and concern for her child, and her decision that her baby should have a family, forever.

It is very important for you to try to understand two big things about the decision *your* birthmother made:

First, whatever kind of life or problems she had, your birthmother did not feel that she could provide what you needed. That's why she arranged for a life she was sure would be better for you.

Second, this decision was probably made before you were even born. It wasn't that your birthmother couldn't take care of you in particular, or that she was unhappy with you for some reason. She just couldn't take care of *any* baby at that time in her life.

There are many adopted kids, maybe even some of your friends. Most of them came to their families because their birthmothers were in similar situations and made choices similar to those your birthmother made.

In Korea, young women who are going to have babies are often fortunate to have a special place to go for help. They might choose to live in a birthmother's home. It's usually a big house with twenty to forty other young women, who are also all waiting for their babies to be born.

In these homes, the mothers get good medical care while their babies are growing inside their bodies and when the babies are born. Even after the birth of their babies, the mothers continue to receive more assistance in carrying out their plans for a new life for their babies. They may also be taught skills that will help them when they leave the birthmother's home, such as how to work with computers or how to sew.

Everyone in the home works together and helps one another. Here they are preparing kimchi, one of the foods Koreans eat with almost every meal.

Being pregnant must be difficult for a birthmother, whether she is alone or in a home with other young women. She can feel her baby growing inside her. She thinks about her baby a lot, hoping that she has made the right decision.

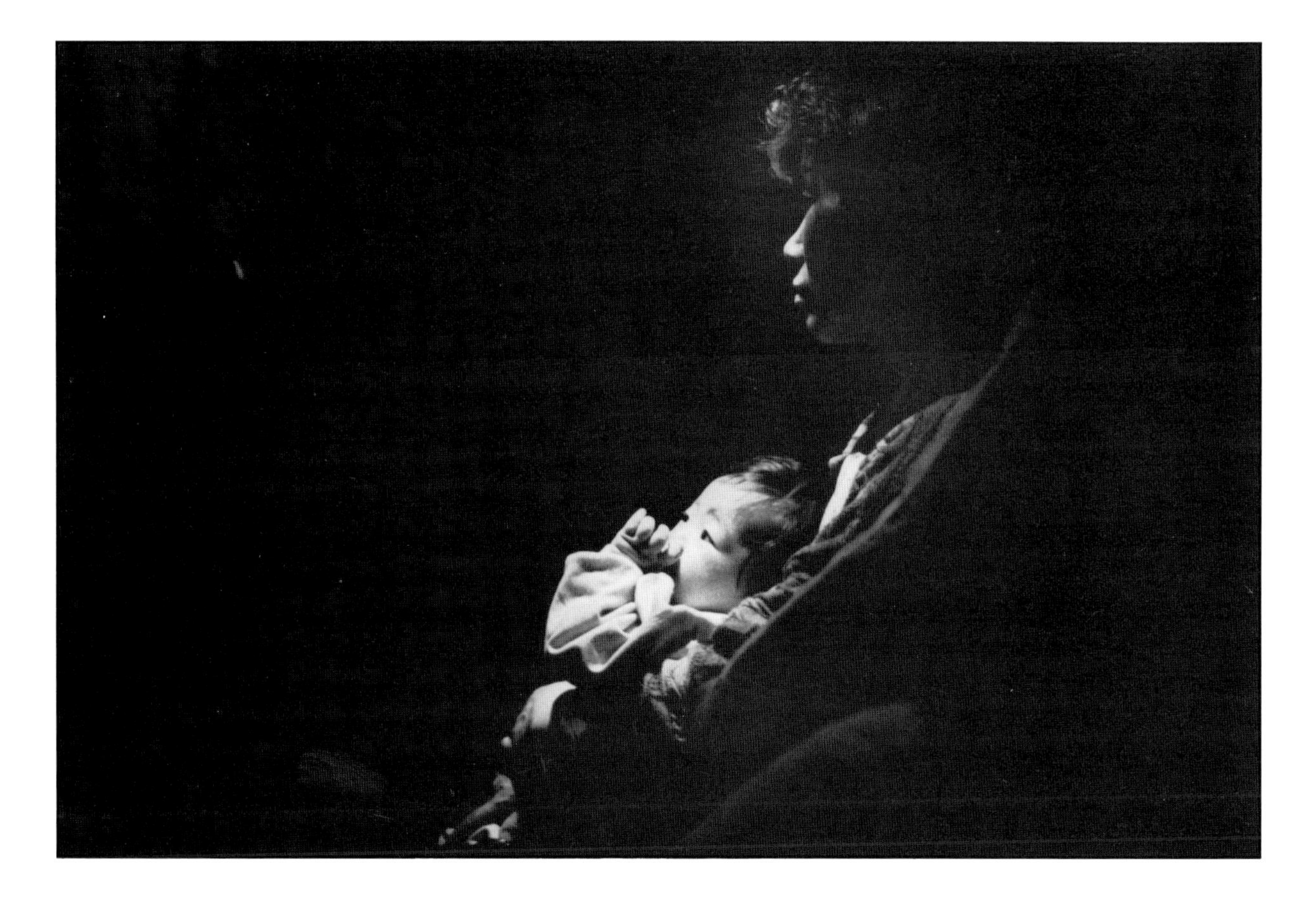

Soon after her baby's birth, she must say good-bye to her child, and put her trust in the social workers. It was very hard for your birthmother to say good-bye to you. It made her very sad, but she knew that you were going to a family who would help you grow and give you love just as she would.

When you were only a few days old, you may have been placed directly into a foster home. If you needed some extra care, you may have come first to a baby's home like this one. Social workers have set up this home to be sure that the newborn babies are truly healthy.

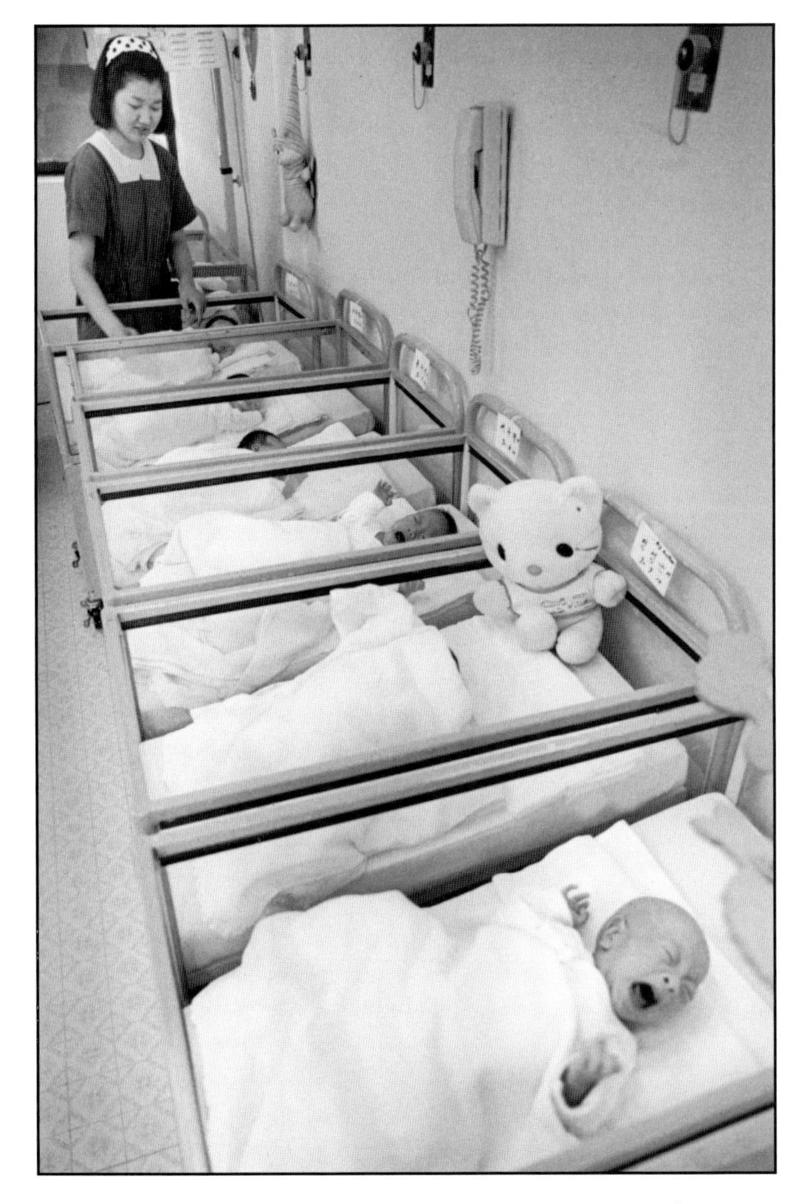

The babies get a chance to grow here. Doctors and nurses watch to be sure that all the babies are healthy and off to a good start.

Much of your time was spent in a crib among many other babies. Sometimes one baby would start crying, because he was hungry and wanted a bottle. All the babies might then start crying at once, and the room would be very noisy.

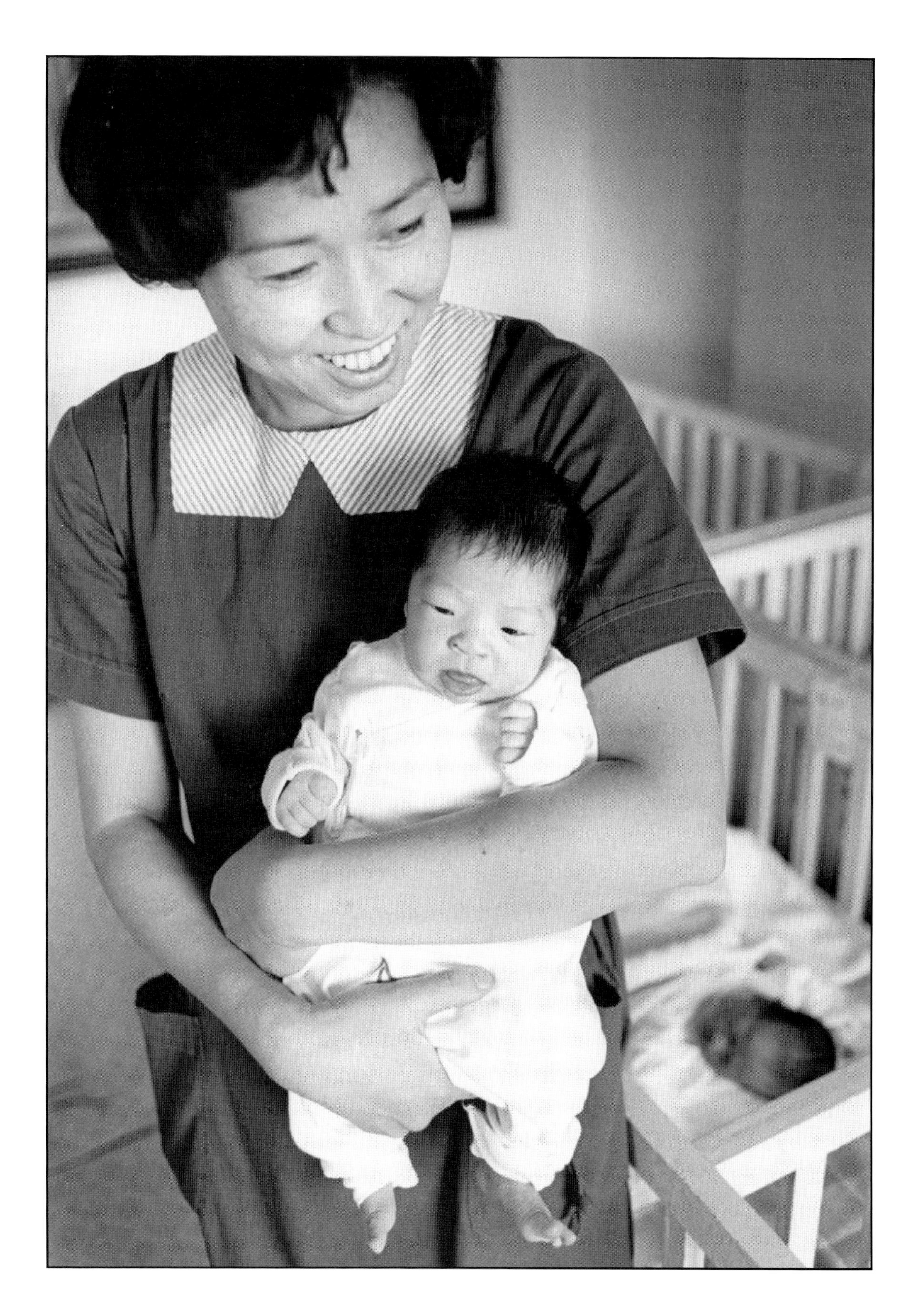

The nurses there were wonderful to you and the other babies. They spent their days holding, feeding, diapering and cuddling the babies.

The nurses knew all the babies by name, and often would sing softly as they cared for each child.

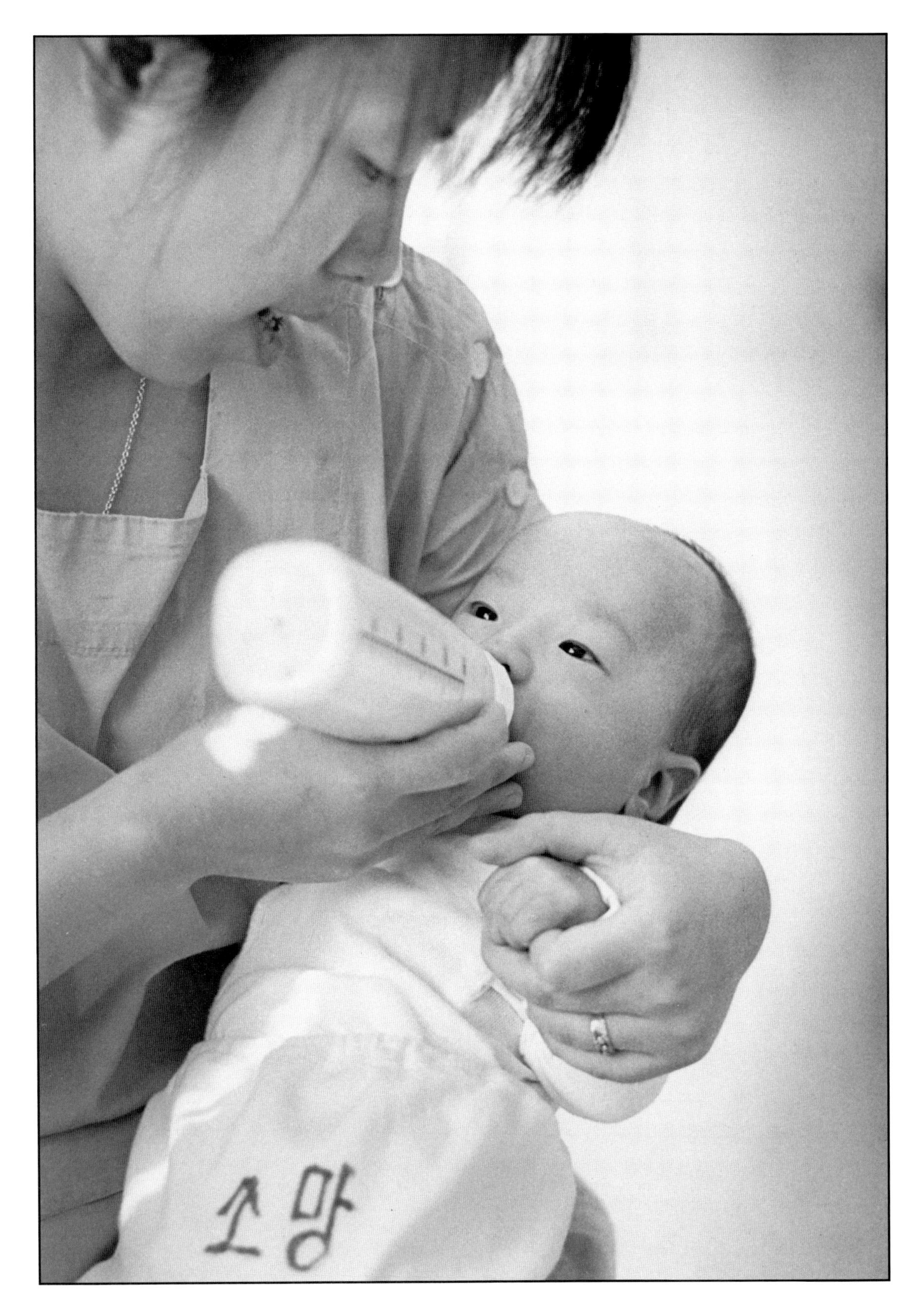

Your days in the baby's home had a regular routine. You had your meals, diaper changes, and some time to roll around on the floor for exercise and play.

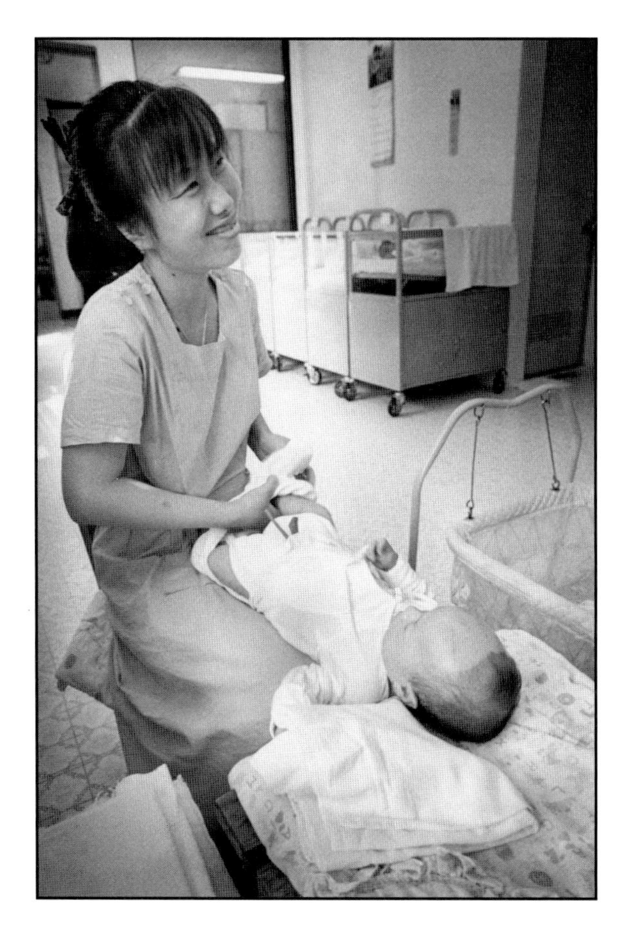

The nurses were always busy with you and the other babies, but it was very satisfying work for them. They knew that they were helping you grow on your way to your new family.

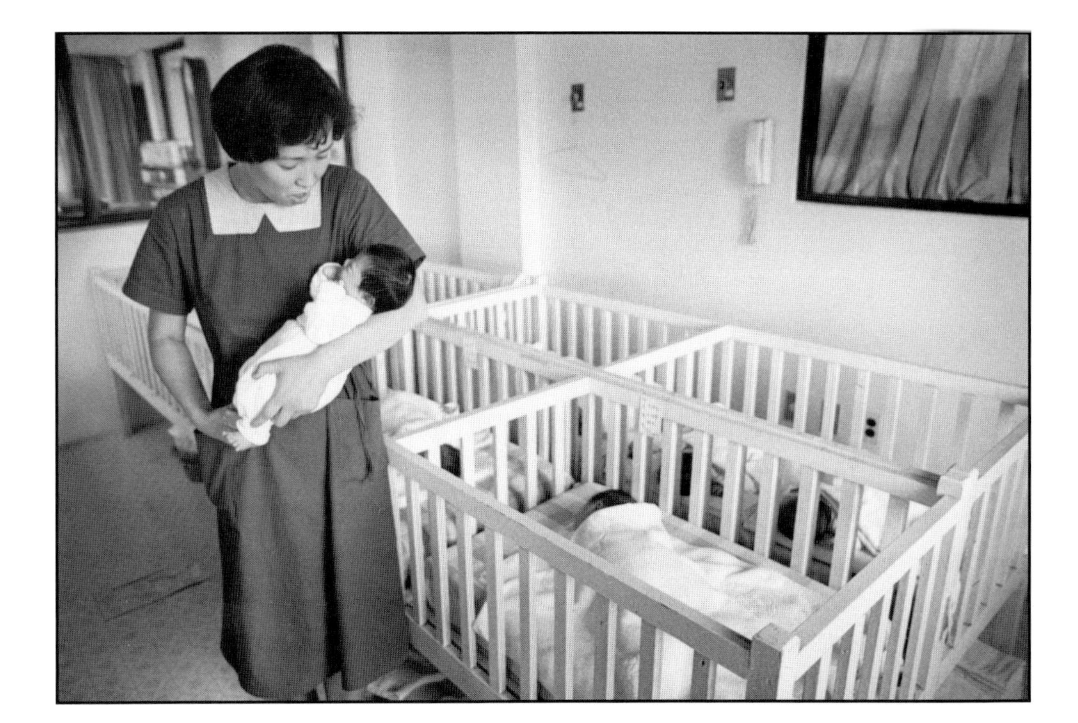

The nurses' jobs certainly weren't over at the end of the day. At night, if you or the other babies were upset or couldn't sleep, they would pick you up and walk you and sing to you.

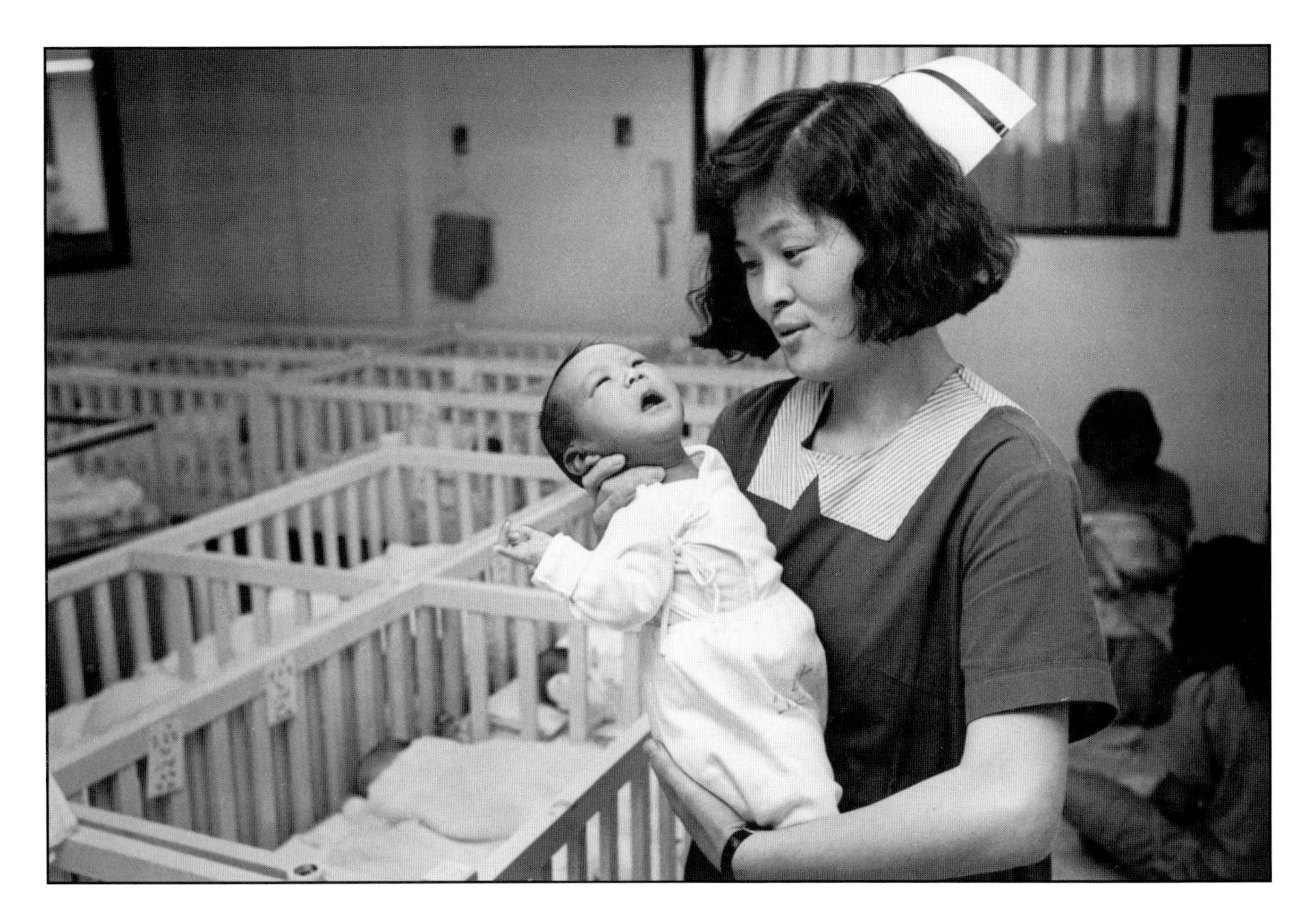

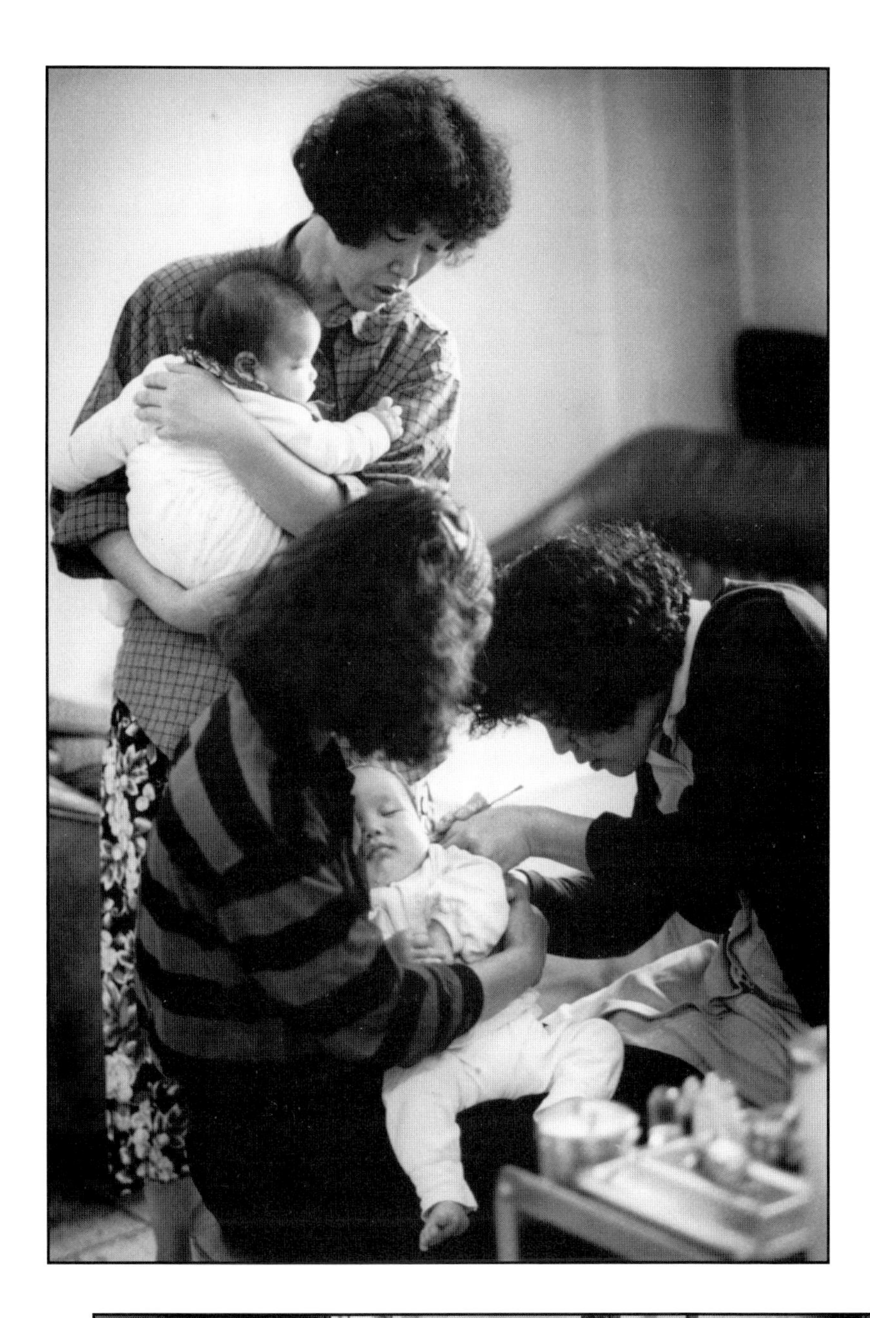

During the time you were in the baby's home, doctors and nurses watched you grow and took good care of you. You were given shots and check-ups and any medicine you may have needed. This baby's home had a whole doctor's office inside it.

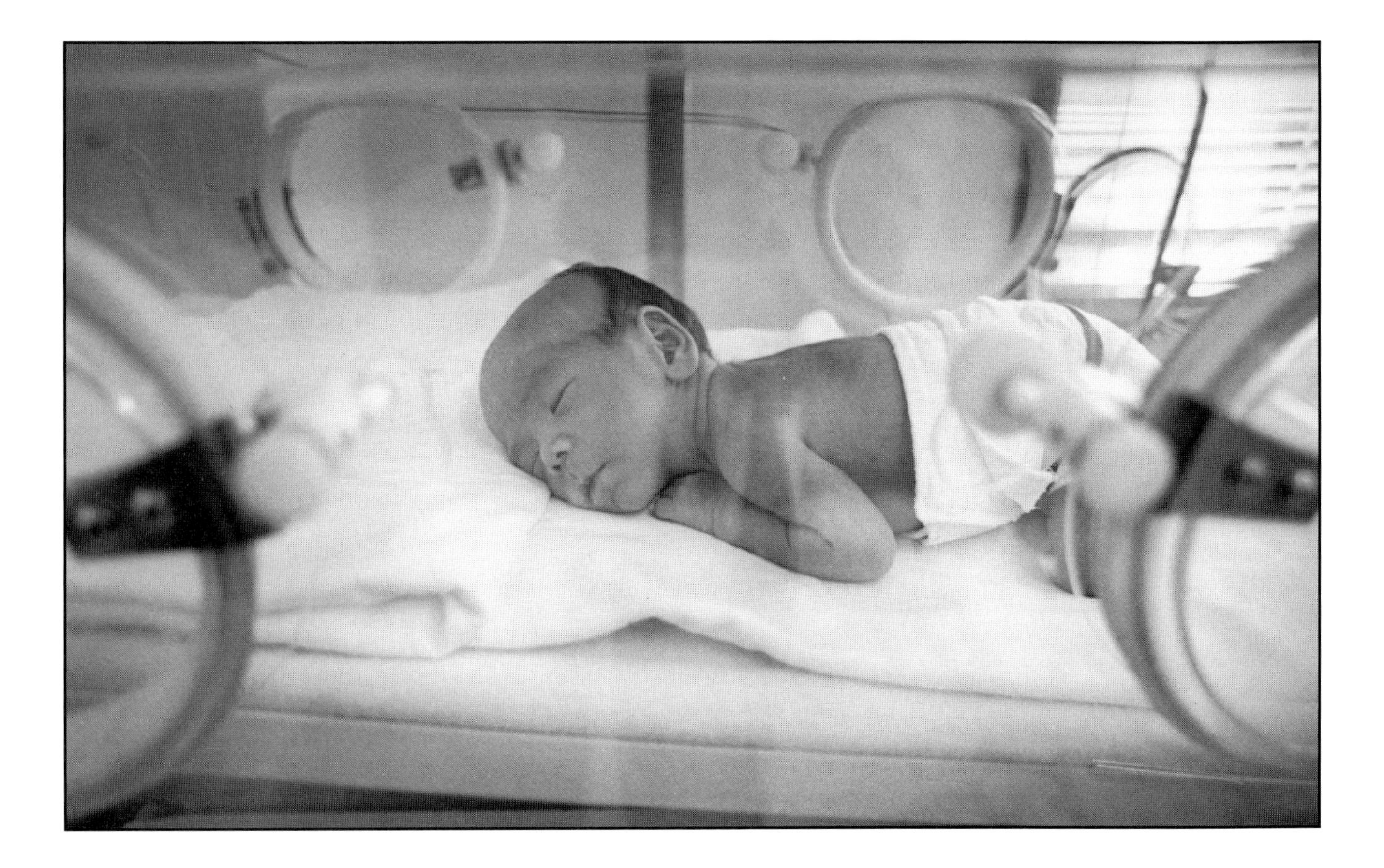

The baby's home also had a small hospital for newborn babies. If you were born a little early, or if you were ill when you came to the baby's home, you would have first stayed here. Some babies had to be in an incubator at first, so that they would be warm and safe and able to grow.

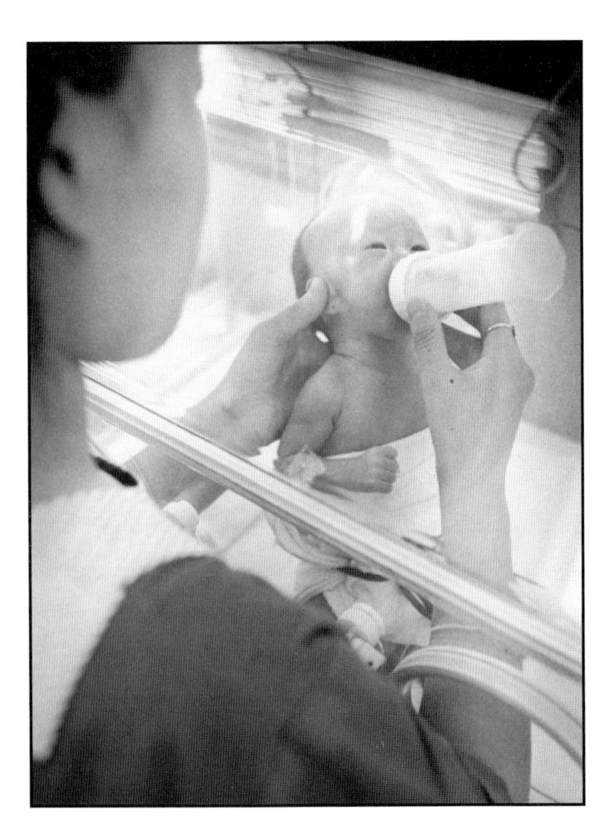

You were probably happy in the baby's home, since the nurses were taking such good care of you. However, the social workers at the adoption agency knew how you could be even more comfortable. They wanted you to live in a home with a nice family until you were ready to be adopted by your parents.

When you first came to the baby's home, a social worker was assigned to you. She had a special interest in you because it was her job to make sure that your birthmother's wishes for you were kept, and that you would have a family of your own.

The doctor told your social worker that you were very healthy, and that you no longer needed the special care you received in the baby's home. She then began to arrange for a foster mother who would take care of you until it was time to go to your new family.

There are many wonderful women who are foster mothers for babies like you. They take care of their foster babies just as if they were their own children, and they come to love them.

They also know that they will be sending their babies to new families, who will take care of them forever. The foster moms are very happy that their babies will soon have families of their own, and this helps them prepare for the time when the babies leave for their new homes.

Your social worker and your foster mother became the two most important people to you at this time of your life. They took over the plan that your birthmother had made for you. By now you were only a month or two old, and many people had played an important part in your life's story.

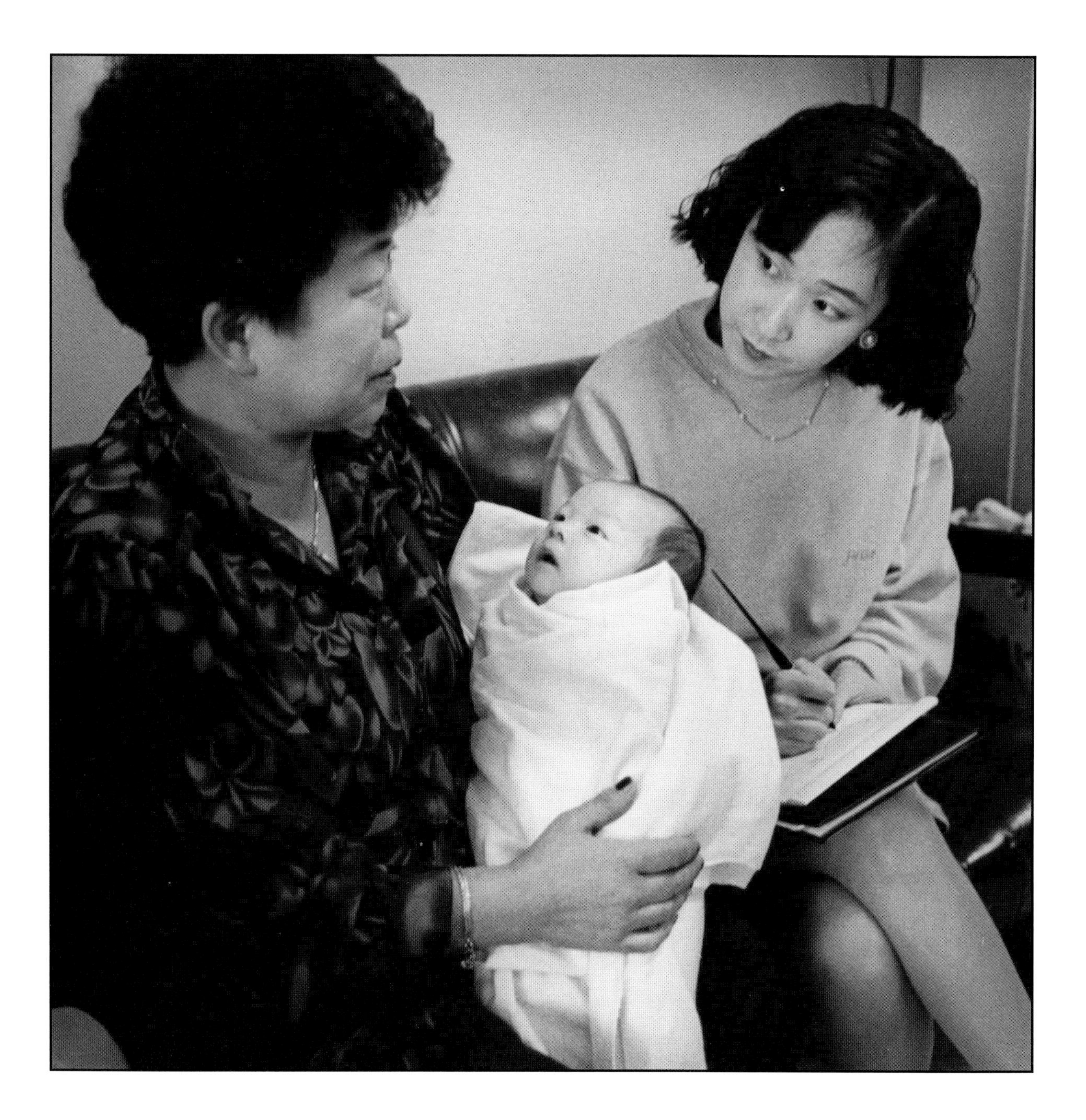

Living with your foster mother was really a whole new experience for you. Now you lived in a regular Korean house or apartment, and became part of your foster family's daily life. You were staying with this family while your social worker arranged the biggest, most important, and final part of the plan for your early life. She was working with other social workers in America to bring you together, forever, with a family who wanted and needed you.

As you did at the baby's home, you soon settled into a regular routine in your foster home. Your foster mother was very busy with her home and family and you. She really loved caring for you. As she went about her chores, your foster mother carried you on her back wrapped in a type of blanket called a *podaegi*. This is how all Korean babies are held and carried when they are small.

Sometimes you went outside with your foster mother, such as when she went shopping for groceries. You were with her as she worked around her home, or prepared meals for her family. Through the day she took good care of you, and she was very happy to have you as a part of her family.

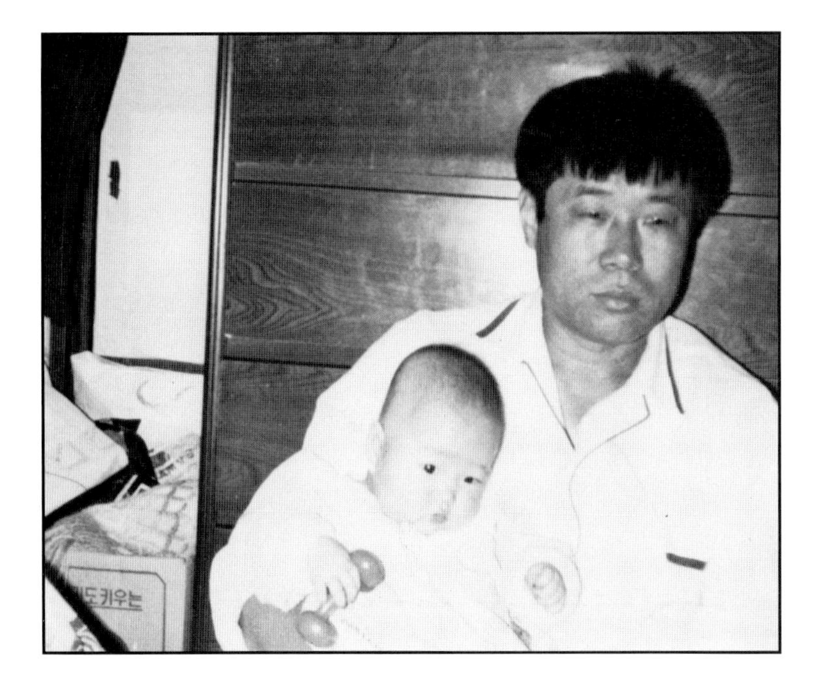

Foster families are very special people. They bring a baby into their home and lives, and give that baby so much love and care. Often there are other children in the family who play with the babies. Foster fathers will get up in the middle of the night when the baby needs some extra attention. There may be other members of the family who join in, too, such as aunts or grandparents.

There were many babies who were living lives very much like yours. They also had birthparents and nurses and social workers and foster mothers. All these people and babies had one place in common: the adoption agency.

This office was always a very busy place. The people at the adoption agency worked hard to make sure that everybody was taken care of, and that all the babies got the help they needed. Many of the people who worked in the adoption agency had something to do with you. They may have helped your social worker, or sent reports to America, or helped distribute milk and supplies, or just made sure that everything was going well for you.

Your foster mother regularly brought you to the adoption agency office. She wanted to talk to your social worker about how you were doing. She also took you to the doctor to be sure that you were healthy and growing. On each visit you were measured and weighed to be sure you were growing well.

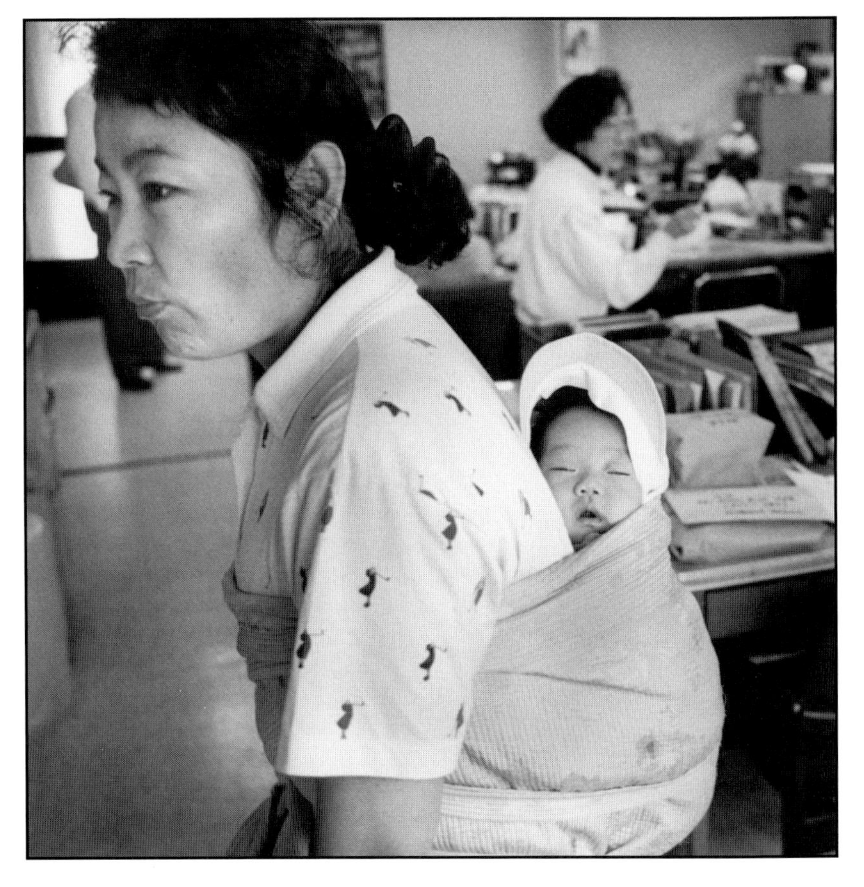

On these check-up visits back to the adoption agency, you saw many other babies and their foster moms. They were also in for their check-ups. When the foster mothers met at the agency, they liked to visit with each other. Your foster mother probably told the others what a wonderful baby you were, because she was very proud of you. She was proud of herself, too, for how well you were growing under her care and attention.

While you were living with your foster mother, your adoption agency in Korea was talking to an adoption agency in America. The American agency had families who really wanted to have a baby join them. The two agencies brought you together with such a family, and made a whole new family, *your* family! Now the most important piece of the plan your birthmother made for you was going to happen.

Adoption is an interesting process. Your birthmother made the difficult decision that she couldn't raise you. At the same time, somewhere else, there was a mom and dad who really needed and wanted to have a baby just like you in their family. Your parents probably have a story of their own to tell, about what it was like before you came to them, and how they felt and what they did. First, though, there is more to the story of your life before you met your mom and dad.

Your social worker told your foster mother that you were now going to join your new family. Your foster mother was both happy and sad. You were a very special baby for her, and she would miss you. At the same time, she felt really happy for you and for your new family, because she knew how special you would be to them, too.

Sometimes, new parents are lucky enough to come to Korea to pick up their baby. They get to meet the foster mother and the social workers, and thank them in person for the wonderful loving care they gave to their child. They are also able to see the country in which their baby was born.

The foster mother is always very excited to meet the parents of the baby she has loved. She feels good that her foster child is going to such nice people. She can share that good feeling with the many other foster mothers who wonder what their foster children's new parents might be like.

Whether at the adoption agency in Korea, or a little later at the airport in America, there is no experience for a mom and dad quite like seeing their new child for the very first time. The day mom and dad first met you will always be a very special day to remember in your family.

Most new families have to hold their excitement for just a few more days, while their baby makes the long airplane trip from Korea.

The day you began your trip to your new home was surely very exciting. Your foster mother and all the social workers and nurses waved good-bye as you got into a van at the adoption agency to leave for the airport. You were held by your escort, the person who would take care of you on the airplane and take you to your new family. There were probably several other children making this trip at the same time as you. They also had some very eager new moms and dads waiting for them to arrive in America.

As they said good-bye to you, your foster mother and all the other people in the adoption agency were sad, since they would miss you.

But they also felt joy and happiness for you: you and the other babies in the van were now on your way to a new life. They had done their part in the plan your birthmother made for you. They were sure you would have a wonderful life with your new family.

When you got to the airport, there was a lot of activity with luggage, and airplane tickets, and official paperwork. As your escort carried you through the airport to the plane, you might have been aware of all these new places and faces.

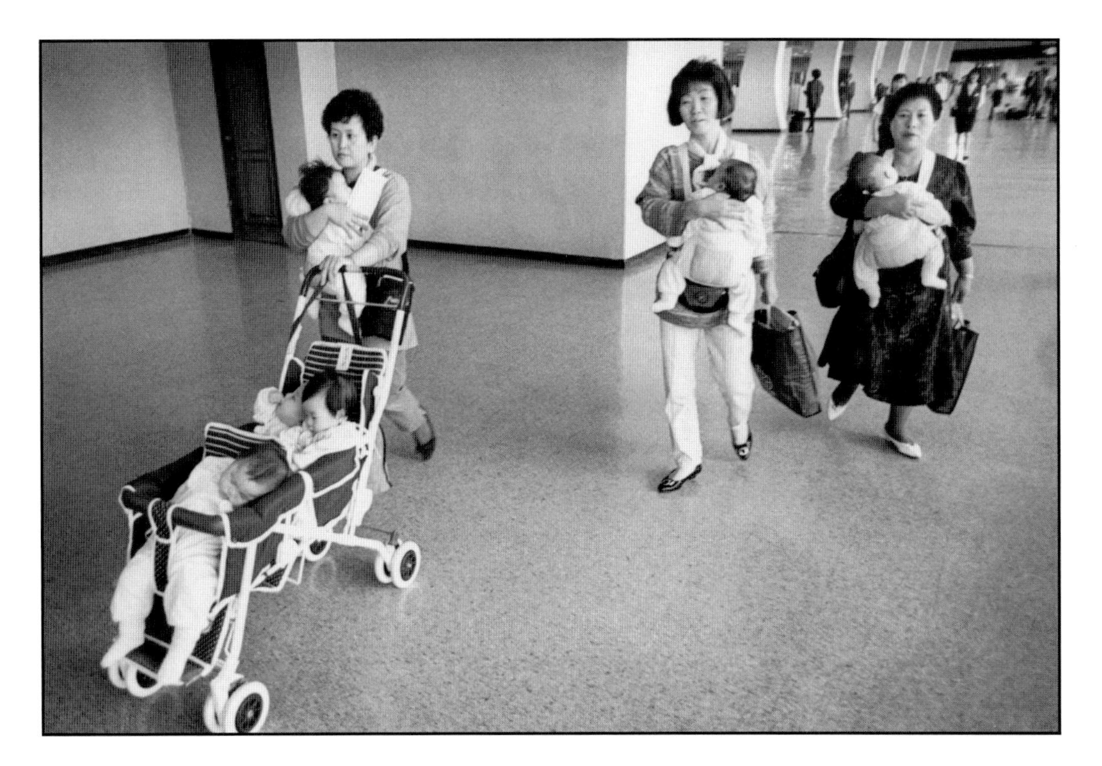

Your airplane was very large. Your escorts took you and the other babies on board the plane before all the other passengers, so that you would have time to get settled and have your bottle. The flight across the ocean to America was going to be very long, so it was good to get comfortable.

Your airplane ride is a very interesting part of your story. Not many babies get to take such a long airplane trip. You were such a tiny baby then, sitting in such a big seat.

You were leaving a country that was your birthplace and your home, and you were going to a new home. You were changing from one life to a new life. You were on a very big journey to your new family.

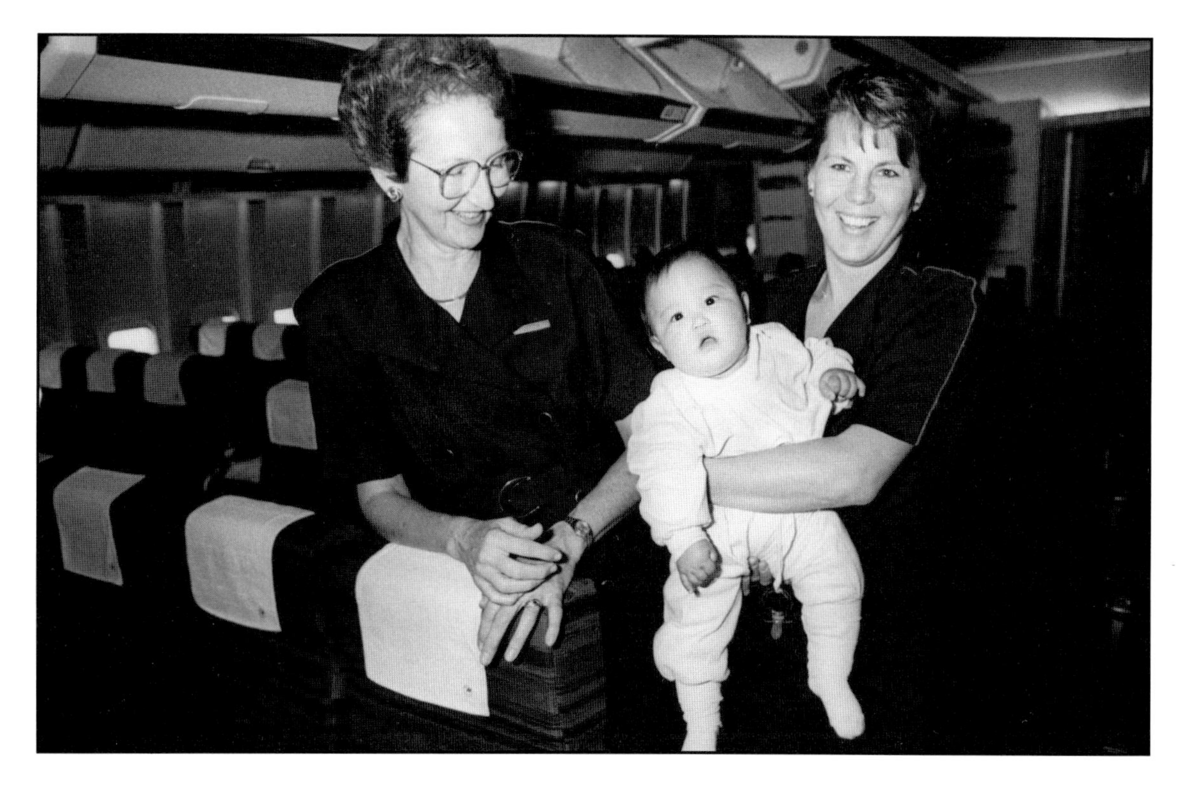

On the airplane, you and the other babies were the centers of attention. Many adults like to help out with babies. Also, most people on the plane were not familiar with Korean adoptions, and they had questions and showed great interest in you. Many of the other passengers just wanted to help the escorts take care of you. The flight attendants usually had seen babies and escorts on their flights before, and they were especially helpful.

The escorts knew that it was their responsibility to get you to your new home. They worked hard through the flight to be sure that you and the other babies were comfortable and received good care.

At last you arrived in America! When your plane landed, some very nice volunteers from the Traveler's Aid Society came on board to take charge of you and the other babies.

When a plane coming from another country first lands in the United States, all its passengers have to pass through Immigration and Customs. The Traveler's Aid people first took you through the Immigration lines, where they showed your Korean passport so you could enter the United States. Then they took you into a nursery to change your clothes and take care of you until your escorts returned from presenting their passports. Again, new people entered your life, though very briefly, to help you on your way to your new family. They were also part of the plan to get you to your mom and dad.

Most of the Korean babies coming to America travel from the first airport to one closer to their new homes. You, too, probably got on another airplane for the last part of your trip.

You waited for your next flight with the Traveler's Aid volunteers. After sitting for so long on the flight from Korea, this was a nice chance for you to stretch and crawl around. When it was time to board the plane, the volunteers said good-bye to you and handed you back to your escort. You then got on the next airplane, and settled in for another flight before you would meet your new family!

All during your long trip, things were happening with your mom and dad. Their social worker told them in advance when you would arrive, and they were getting more and more excited. Not only your parents, but your whole new family was gathering at the airport with balloons and cameras and presents. They just couldn't wait for your plane to land and for the doors to open and for you to come out!

At last, your plane arrived. You were brought off the airplane and placed in the arms of your mom and dad.

You probably have your own pictures of your arrival, and you can see how happy and thrilled your whole family was.

No one at the airport could have been as happy as your mom and dad.

Here you are at last, in the arms of your new parents. Behind you are the wonderful people in Korea who helped you along the way. You started with your birthparents, especially your birthmother, who gave birth to you and chose this life for you, making the plan that brought you to your family. Your foster mother, the social workers, the doctors and nurses, and so many others had a part in caring for you and in bringing you to your mom and dad.

Many of those people back in Korea think of you still.

May you keep them in your heart as you grow.

You've come to us from so far away, and so many wonderful people have helped you get here.

We are so glad to have you.

Welcome home.

Brian Boyd and Stephen Wunrow are both parents of children from Korea. Brian is a sales manager for a large publisher, and Steve is a freelance photographer. They each have two adorable kids, and both are still happily married despite spending an inordinate amount of time on this book. The authors are similarly matched in their ability to consume with pleasure large quantities of kimchi, a taste for which they acquired on their visits to Korea.

The authors' children (clockwise from upper left):
Sarah Po-Yeong Boyd, Madeleine Soon Young Vickery Wunrow,
Emma Elizabeth Vickery Wunrow, Anna Soo-Yeong Boyd.